mheducation.com/prek-12

Copyright ©2021 McGraw Hill

Send all inquiries to:
McGraw Hill
8787 Orion Place
Columbus, OH 43240

ISBN: 978-1-264-51306-2
MHID: 1-264-51306-2

Printed in the United States of America

1 2 3 4 5 6 7 8 9 LCM 24 23 22 21

Moments for MySELf

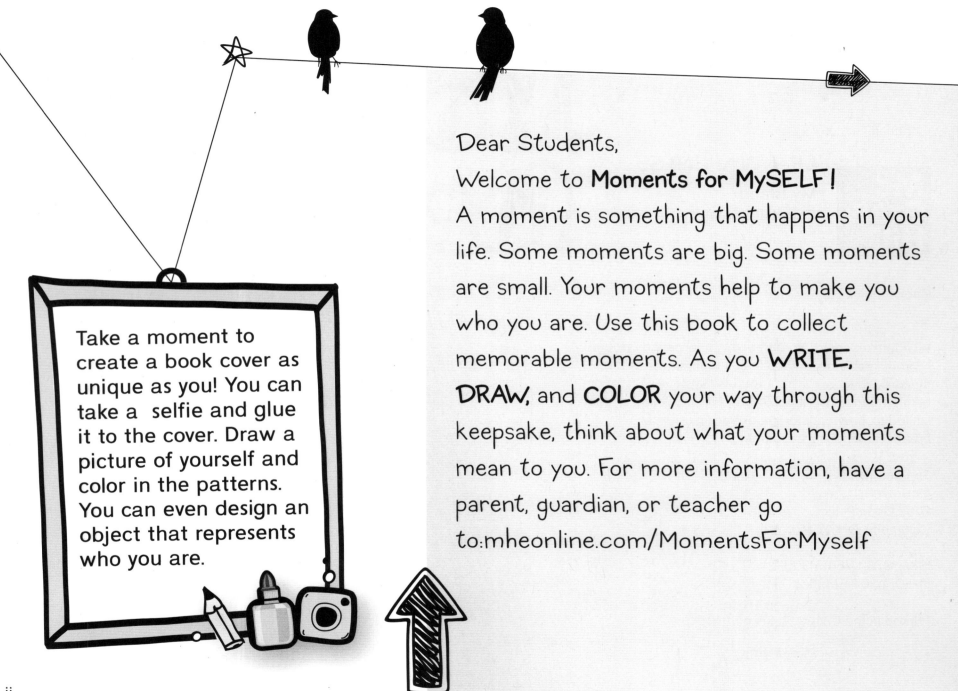

Take a moment to create a book cover as unique as you! You can take a selfie and glue it to the cover. Draw a picture of yourself and color in the patterns. You can even design an object that represents who you are.

Dear Students,

Welcome to **Moments for MySELF!**

A moment is something that happens in your life. Some moments are big. Some moments are small. Your moments help to make you who you are. Use this book to collect memorable moments. As you **WRITE, DRAW,** and **COLOR** your way through this keepsake, think about what your moments mean to you. For more information, have a parent, guardian, or teacher go to:mheonline.com/MomentsForMyself

TABLE OF CONTENTS

p1-10 SELF-AWARENESS

☐ My Island
☐ Colorful Emotions
☐ I Am A Rock Star
☐ Train My Brain
☐ Foldable

p11-20 SELF-MANAGEMENT

☐ Keeping My Cool
☐ Gettable Goal
☐ A Cupful of Courage
☐ Making My Day
☐ Foldable

p21-30 SOCIAL AWARENESS

☐ Someone Else's Shoes
☐ My Thankful Tree
☐ Celebrating Our Differences
☐ I Know How To:
☐ Foldable

p31-40 RELATIONSHIP SKILLS

☐ Everybody Talks
☐ Super Friends
☐ Bubbling Up
☐ I Am A Leader
☐ Foldable

p41-50 RESPONSIBLE DECISION-MAKING

☐ Be Flexible
☐ Penny, Quarter, Dollar Problems
☐ Making Good Choices
☐ I Am Responsible
☐ Foldable

MY ISLAND

Favorite Food Forest

You are special! There is only one of you. The things you feel, say, and do make you who you are.

Create your own island that describes who you are and what makes you special. Fill in all the empty places on the island with words and pictures that describe you. You may **WRITE**, **COLOR**, or **GLUE** pictures to your island.

My Sea of Colors

 Things I Love Villiage

 Things I Can Do Mountains

Friendship
Lagoon

Family
Beach

CHECK IN ✓ **CIRCLE** the emoji that matches how you are feeling, or **DRAW** your own.

2

Colorful Emotions

Emotions are also called feelings. We all have them. Happiness, worry, and love are some of the many feelings we have. Feelings help us understand who we are.

What color are your emotions?

COLOR each feeling.

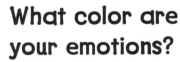

silly

worried

mad

sad

happy

DRAW a face that shows one of your emotions. **WRITE** the word for your emotion below.

_____

 **WRITE** what happens when you feel this way.

_____

_____

_____

_____

CHECK IN **CIRCLE** the monster that matches how you are feeling, or **DRAW** your own.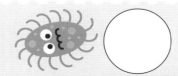

I AM A ROCK STAR

It is important to believe in yourself and think positive thoughts. When you do, it's called being confident. When you are confident you are more ready to handle things that come your way!

Did you know that you are a rock star? Fill the star up with compliments about yourself. You may **WRITE**, **DRAW**, or **GLUE** pictures to your star.

CHECK IN ✓

CIRCLE the weather that matches how you are feeling, or **DRAW** your own.

Bookmark this page so that you can come back to it for a little boost of confidence!

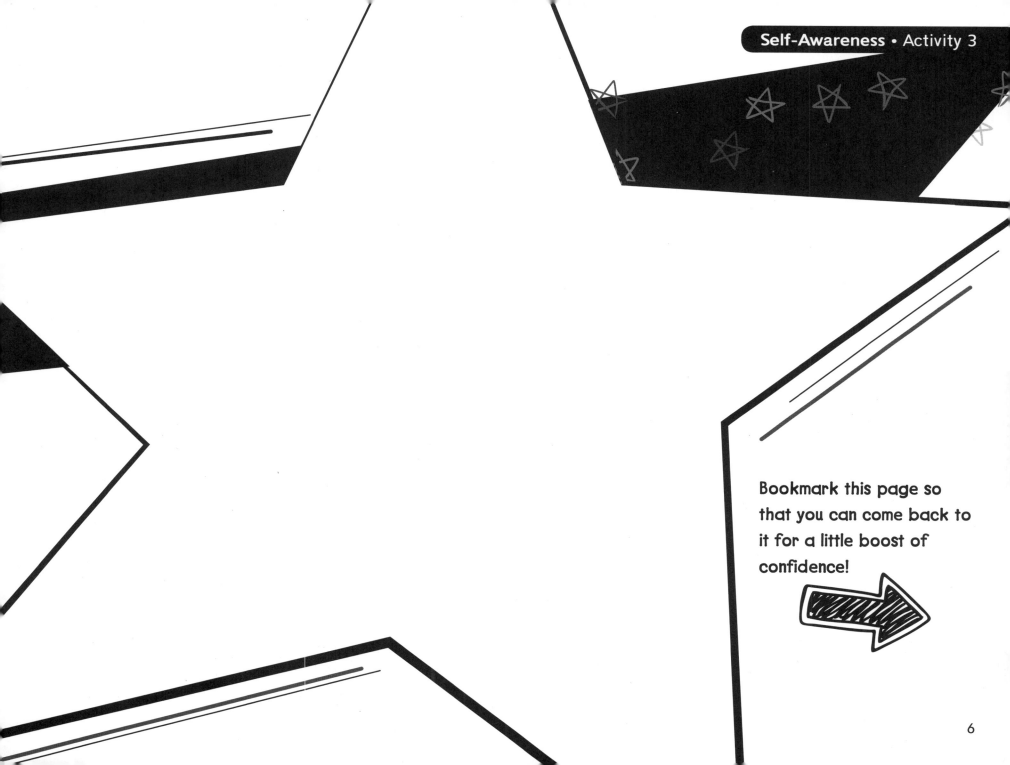

Train My Brain

It's time to train your brain. That's right. You can make your brain stronger by believing in yourself. It's called having a growth mindset. When you believe that you can get better at something by trying hard, you are training your brain for success.

The word yet is important to keep in your brain in order to have a growth mindset.

 **CIRCLE** the instrument that matches how you are feeling, or **DRAW** your own.

DRAW or **WRITE** something you can already do that you are very proud of.

DRAW or **WRITE** something you can't do yet, but you could if you worked hard at it.

Come back to this page from time to time. How are you training your brain for success?

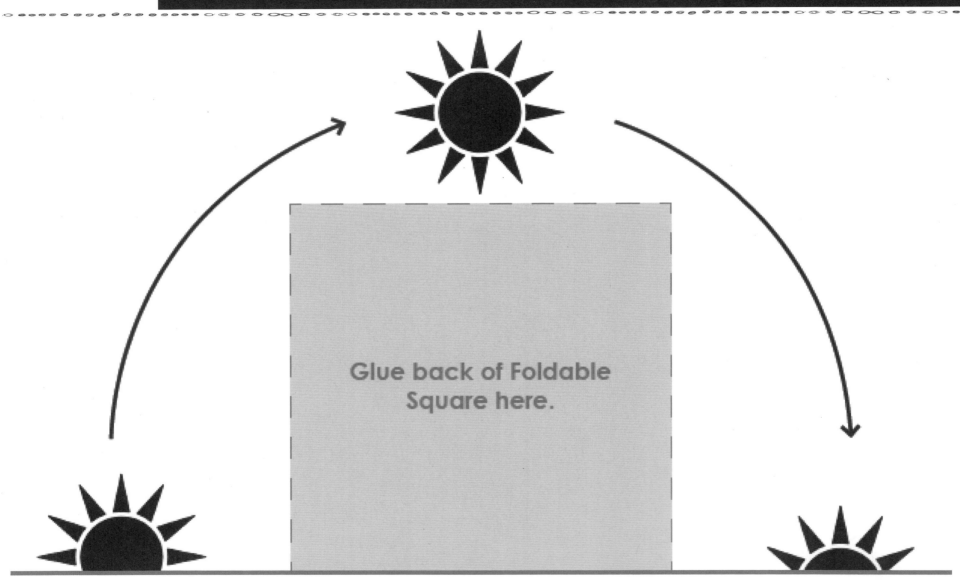

Glue back of Foldable
Square here.

9

Glue anchor tab here.

My Moments

Under the tabs WRITE or DRAW feelings and actions that make you special.

Keeping My Cool

Having self-control means being in charge of what you say and do. You use self-control to keep safe, stay healthy, and create peace.

Learning to control what you say and do takes time and practice. **WRITE** or **DRAW** how you can keep your cool when you are feeling out of control.

CHECK IN ✓

CIRCLE the emoji that matches how you are feeling, or **DRAW** your own.

GETTABLE GOAL

A goal is something you want to make happen.
Goals help you grow and build confidence.
Goals take work, but you can do it!
Planning the steps and taking action
will help you reach your goal.

Think of one goal you wish to make happen. It could be something you want to work on getting better at. It could be finishing your work on time or starting a new sport. Make a plan for getting to your goal.

CHECK IN

CIRCLE the monster that matches how you are feeling, or **DRAW** your own.

   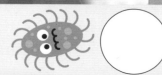

1 My Goal

2 Actions To Take

3 I Can Check My Progress By

4 My Goal Will Be Completed By

A CUPEFUL OF COURAGE

Your courage comes from your heart. It helps you to do the right thing even when it is not easy. There are many ways to show courage. You can try something new, overcome a challenge, or tell someone how you feel. How do you show courage?

WRITE and **DRAW** how you show courage.

CHECK IN ✓

CIRCLE the weather that matches how you are feeling, or **DRAW** your own.

15

I SHOW COURAGE BY

Making My Day

How organized are you? Being organized allows you to come up with a plan and follow through to get work done. Checklists are a tool that can help you stay organized.

What routine is hardest for you? Morning or night? Create a checklist to help you organize your tasks.

Use your checklist to help you through your routine!

CIRCLE the instrument that matches how you are feeling, or DRAW your own.

WRITE task   **DRAW Description**   **FILL IN the time of day**

Color one

👍👎 taking a deep breath.

👍👎 asking for help.

👍👎 taking a break.

👍👎 counting to 10.

Color one

👍👎 do the right thing.

👍👎 do new things.

👍👎 talk about my feelings.

Color one

👍👎 I can reach.

👍👎 make me a better person!

Glue anchor tab here.
Self-Management

Today

Think about your day.

Read the sentences below.

Use the card to answer Yes or No.

Do this on different days.

Do your answers change?

Glue Pocket Strip tab here to hold card.

● Today I showed self control.

● Today I had courage.

● Today I set a goal.

● Today I felt organized.

20

Someone Else's Shoes

Empathy is being able to think about and understand how others are feeling. It is being able to imagine how you might feel if the same thing happened to you. Sometimes we call empathy being able to "put yourself in someone else's shoes."

Take a moment to think about something difficult that happened to a friend or family member.

How are you feeling?

I understand how you feel.

I am here to listen.

DRAW or **WRITE** what you would say to your friend or family member to help them feel better.

☺ I would say:

DRAW or **WRITE** about how you would feel if the same thing happened to you.

☺ I would feel:

How can I help?

CHECK IN

CIRCLE the emoji that matches how you are feeling, or **DRAW** your own.

22

Gratitude is when you take time to appreciate and be thankful for the good things in your life. You can be thankful for your family and friends, the fun things you get to do, and the things you have.

My Thankful Tree

 **CHECK IN**

CIRCLE the monster that matches how you are feeling, or **DRAW** your own.

   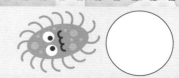

CUT and **GLUE** pictures of all the things you are grateful for in your life.

_____'s

Thankful Tree

CELEBRATING OUR Differences

It's important to treat everyone with kindness and respect, no matter how different they are from us. We can learn from each other when we celebrate what is different about us.

This is me!

This is _____!

Choose a friend to work with. **WRITE** or **DRAW** what is the same and what is different about one another.

Ways we are alike:

What I love about my friend!

Ways we are different:

What I love about me!

CIRCLE the weather that matches how you are feeling, or **DRAW** your own.

I Know How To:

Part of learning and growing is knowing how to behave around others. There are so many rules for behaving at school, at home, and in your community.

← **Use Manners**

Follow Directions →

CHECK IN ✓

CIRCLE the instrument that matches how you are feeling, or DRAW your own.

27

How can you show others you know how to behave?
WRITE or **DRAW** a rule for each How To statement.

Be Patient

Use Kind Words

Say Hello

On the front tabs, DRAW a picture for each social awareness skill. Under the tabs, WRITE about each skill.

Glue back of Four-Door Shutter Foldable here.

Glue pocket edges here.

Glue pocket edges here.

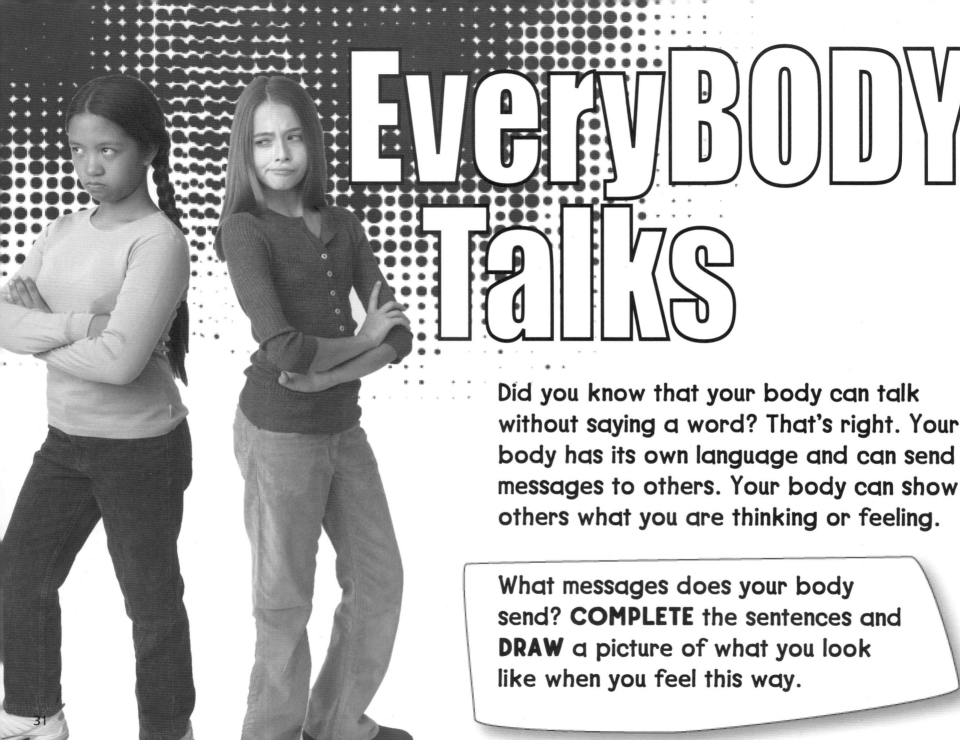

EveryBODY Talks

Did you know that your body can talk without saying a word? That's right. Your body has its own language and can send messages to others. Your body can show others what you are thinking or feeling.

What messages does your body send? **COMPLETE** the sentences and **DRAW** a picture of what you look like when you feel this way.

31

When I feel _____

my body looks like this:

When someone _____

I feel _____.

My body looks like this:

CHECK IN ✓

CIRCLE the emoji that matches how you are feeling, or **DRAW** your own.

SUPER FRIENDS

A good friend is someone who cares about you. A person you can trust, have fun with, and is kind. Good friends listen to each other and help you when you are in need.

What do you look for in a good friend? **WRITE** or **DRAW** 3 things that make someone a good friend.

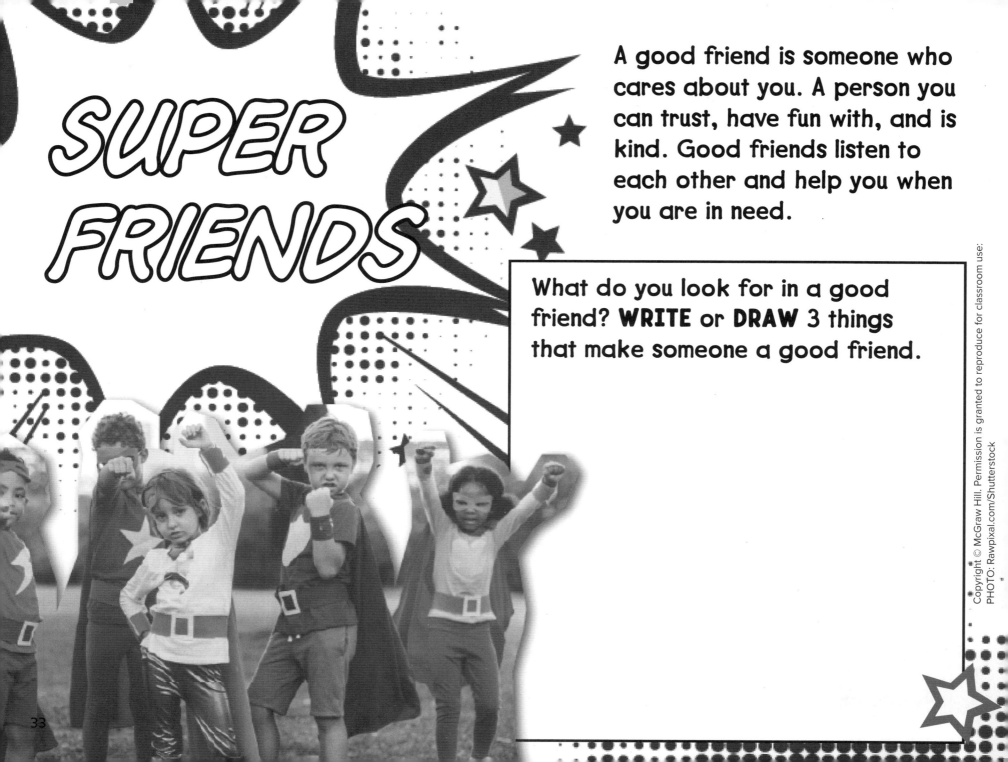

Mark a square for each time you are a good friend. Can you get 3 in a row?

Listen to a friend.	Share with a friend.	Play a game a friend wants to play.
Help a friend.	Show kindness to a friend.	Keep a promise to a friend.
Give a compliment to a friend.	Make a new friend feel welcome.	Take turns with a friend.

CIRCLE the monster that matches how you are feeling, or **DRAW** your own.

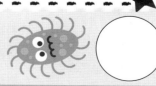

BUBBLING UP

A conflict is a disagreement between people. Conflicts happen to everyone. When they do, it's important to stay calm. Before you can make things better, you need to use your thinking brain. A thinking brain is a calm brain. It helps you make better decisions.

CIRCLE the weather that matches how you are feeling, or **DRAW** your own.

What are ways that you can calm down when your emotions start to bubble up? **DRAW** or **WRITE** strategies that you can use when you are upset.

I Am A Leader

A leader is someone that shows us how to act. We look up to them! Some leaders teach us how to make good choices. Anyone can be a leader! You have the makings of a great leader.

What makes a good leader? WRITE down ways you think good leaders should act, things they should say, and thoughts they may have.

Act    **Say**    **Think**

CHECK IN   CIRCLE the instrument that matches how you are feeling, or DRAW your own.

38

Read the sentences on the tabs. DRAW pictures under the tabs to show each skill.

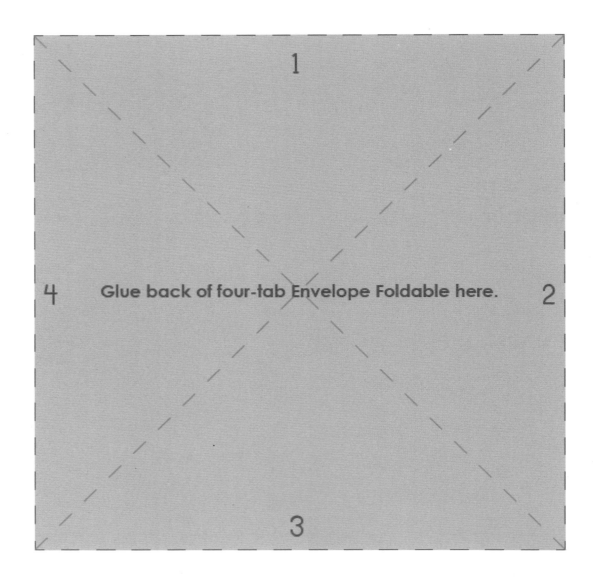

1

4   Glue back of four-tab Envelope Foldable here.   2

3

DRAW a picture of a conflict or disagreement. Under the picture, DRAW or WRITE ways you can stay calm when you feel upset.

Glue bottom back of the Standing Display Foldable here.

BE FLEXIBLE

Change can be scary and can make you feel upset. But change is okay! When change happens, it is important to think flexibly.

Thinking flexibly is when you are able to think about something in a new way. When you think flexibly you can handle changes in school or with your friends better.

Sometimes things may not go as planned. **WRITE** a Do and Don't list to help you be flexible when plans change.

PLAN FOR CHANGE

DO
Keep an open mind

DON'T
Be afraid of new things

_____

_____

_____

_____

 **CHECK IN** — **CIRCLE** the emoji that matches how you are feeling, or **DRAW** your own.

Everyone has problems! When you have a problem, you need to figure out how to solve it. To solve a problem, first figure out what the problem is. Then, figure out the size of the problem. Once you know how big it is, you can figure out what to do next.

Penny, Quarter, Dollar Problems

Problems come in different shapes and sizes. **DRAW** or **WRITE** an example of a penny, quarter, and dollar problem. **EXPLAIN** how you would solve each problem.

CHECK IN

CIRCLE the monster that matches how you are feeling, or **DRAW** your own.

43

Penny Problems:
small problems that are
frustrating and no one is
in danger or breaking
any rules

Quarter Problems:
medium problems when you
need help or someone is
breaking a rule

Dollar Problems:
big problems that
are an emergency
and are
dangerous

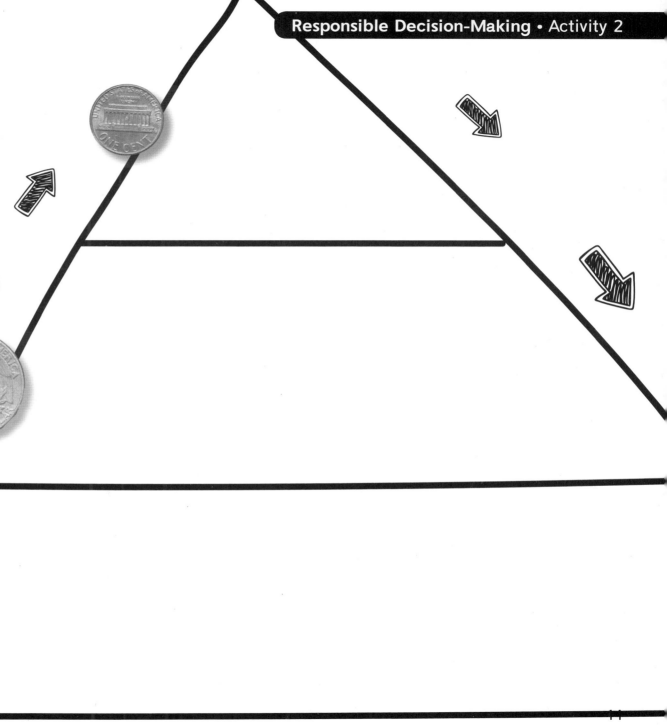

Making Good Choices

Every day you are faced with choices. The choices you make have consequences. A consequence is something that happens as the result of something. Some consequences are good and some are not. It all depends on the choices YOU make.

You put your toys away. They are safe.

You leave your toys out. They get stepped on and break.

Good choices keep you safe, healthy, and happy. Good choices have good consequences. **WRITE** a list of 3 good choices that you will make at school or at home this week.

1 _____

2 _____

3 _____

Use the crystal ball to **DRAW** what your future will look like when you make these good choices.

 **CHECK IN** **CIRCLE** the weather that matches how you are feeling, or **DRAW** your own.

46

I AM RESPONSIBLE

Being responsible means doing the things that you are supposed to do. When you are responsible, you take care of yourself and others. You choose to do the right thing at the right time, so others can trust and depend on you.

DRAW or **WRITE** about how you are responsible.

CIRCLE the instrument that matches how you are feeling, or **DRAW** your own.

I am responsible to myself by:

I am responsible at home by:

I am responsible to my community by:

I am responsible at school by:

Store your cards in the pocket strip below. Use them to WRITE or DRAW examples of thinking flexibly, making good choices, being responsible, and solving problems.

Glue the Pocket Strip tab here to hold cards.

A picture of me making
a good choice.

Glue back of Half-Book Foldable here.

Moments With Friends

AHA Moments

Moments to Remember